woodstock 94

(W) Love, Peace, Harmony and where is my fucking tent?[*]

FOREWORD > > > The road to Woodstock '94 for me began by spending a
agitated and middle-aged father screaming, "You spent $441 on what?"
perspective on the big event. My hairdresser compares it to her leftover
religious woman down the street insists it signals the end of the world. S
stuff, mega-moshing and the Surreal Field. Others say it will never be l
pills. But Woodstock '94 isn't supposed to be a carbon copy: It's the conc

...ling Ticketmaster until my fingers were little stubs. It ended with my very
...speration and disbelief in his voice sums up the general attitude and
...nner. A graying coworker says it reminds him of "Brady Bunch" reruns, and a
...by boomers say Woodstock '94 is just a little too weird — all this cyber-
...e first Woodstock — all that mud, flower power, free sex and rainbow-colored
...uniting a generation that remains. Every generation searches for an

3   3

8   KODAK 505

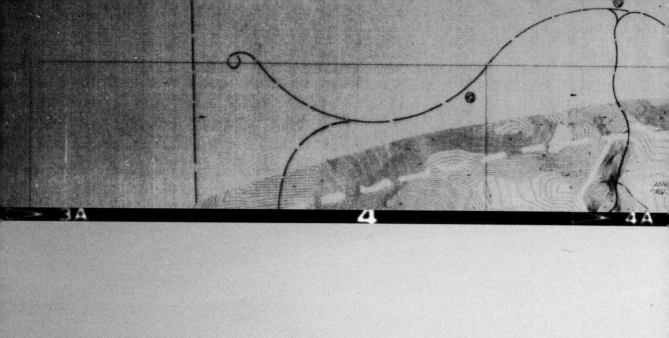

experience it can pass on to the next. For my parents, it was JFK, the m
Woodstock. For us it is racial disunity, a narrow job market and grunge.
writing bad poetry, but we were born too late to experience an event that
felt like Robert Cohn of Ernest Hemingway's novel THE SUN ALSO RISES, who b
a trip like that," Cohn says. "I'll be too old before I can ever do it."
like planning a trip to the moon - we're scared, excited and anxious, but

WOODSTO
August 13th & 14
Saugerties, Ne
30129
General Admi

2 M
D.
of Pl
& M

nding, the Beatles on "The Ed Sullivan Show" and, of course, the original
ew up reading about Woodstock's three days of peace and music, moshing and
y defined a generation but, more important, unified it. At times I have
s pal Jake to go to South America with him. "All my life I've wanted to go on
me that trip is Woodstock '94, and going to Woodstock for my generation is
ast we're going together. A Woodstock nation is not a crazy notion in 1994,

DSTOCK 94

st 13th & 14th, 1994

gerties, New York

301291

General Admission $135.00

2 MORE
DAYS
of PEACE
& MUSIC

nor is it just money, money, money. It is something we can talk about w
make history again," another woman said. She had traded her entire b
freedom. In Michael Cunningham's novel A HOME AT THE END OF THE WORLD, Bo
finds his Woodstock, but for three days this August a new generation of yo

de. "I just want to say I was there," a friend said. "I think it will
count for a ticket, and she waved it around as if it were her ticket to
ends his whole life trying to find the town called Woodstock. Bobby never
ople will.   AMY WU

IF YOU ASK ONE HUNDRE

WOODSTOCK 94 YOU WOULD GET ONE HUNDRE

I WOULD RATHER FIN

I WOULD LIKE TO LOOK AROUND ME AND GET A FE

IF YOU START LISTENING TO WHA

eople what they thought of

fferent opinions.

y own opinion. That is why I am here.

r what this is all about.

her people tell you about Woodstock

you are lost already. Lars Ulrich of Metallica

Backstage Portraits of the Performers
by Albert WAtson

Foreword by AMy WU
essays by John Milward +
christopher John FArley

contributions by Aerosmith
MelisSA Etheridge

Odstock 94
BOok Henry ROllins
+ Green DAy
Afterword by the Producers of WOOdstock

PolyGram diVerSified Entertainment
CallaWay Editions

1994

the b

Abba Rage **Aerosmith**

Allman Brothers Band

Arrested Development

THE BAND'S Big Pink Review

featuring performances by Bob Weir and Rob Wasserman, Roger McGuinn, Hot Tuna + Bruce Hornsby

Blind Melon

Blues Traveler

Candlebox

Jimmy Cliff's Reggae Jam

featuring Diana King, Worl-A-Girl, Toots, Eek-A-Mouse

Joe Cocker

Collective Soul

the Cranberries

Crosby, Stills and Nash

Sheryl Crow

Cypress Hill

Del Amitri

Bob Dylan

Futu Futu

Peter Gabriel

Goat

Green Day

Jackyl

James

and

SPIN

Melissa Etheridge 1992 and 1993 Metallica

The Neville Brothers

Nine Inch Nails

Slash

Primus

Porno for Pyros

Deee-lite

Orleans Peace Bowl

RAVESTOCK featuring Orb, Orbital, Orbital.

Red Hot Chili Peppers

Paul Rodgers'

Rock + Blues Review

featuring Slash, Neil Schon, Jason Bonham, Andy Fraser

Rekk + Roguish Armament

Rollins Band

Salt N' Pepa

Santana

Gil Scott-Heron John Sebastian

The Sisters of Glory featuring Thelma Houston, CeCe Peniston,

Phoebe Snow, Mavis Staples, Lois Walden

Spin Doctors

Three Traffic Vinx

Violent Femmes

W.O.M.A.D. @WOODSTOCK

featuring Xalam, the Justin Trio, Geoffrey Oryema, Hassan Hakmoun

Youssou N'Dour Zucchero

It was a bright and sunny Friday afternoon,

August 12, a full 24 hours before sheets of rain would transform Woodstock '94 into Mudstock II. Huge, white, tubular misting tents set up to cool the crowd in the belly of the 90-acre field facing the massive north stage had already made the surrounding turf wet and soggy. It was this moist bed of

preeminent symbol of "Woodstock '94: The Mud People" — a family of ecstatic music fans who had the anonymous, wigged-out look of the natives in "Apocalypse Now." Historians will debate whether the original Mud Person was born of an accidental slip in the sod or by a theatrical desire to recreate a memorable image from the movie of the original festival. Regardless, as soon as others joined the clan of Mud People running joyfully between the baptismal puddle and the mosh pit in front of the stage, the first vivid connection was made between the fabled festival at Yasgur's Farm and the silver anniversary celebration at Winston Farm.

It would not be the last, for as tens of thousands continued to stream into the site, many of them without tickets, it became clear that Woodstock '94, like its predecessor, was tripping off into a world of its own. The chain-link fence surrounding the 840-acre farm had virtually become an open door, and rules banning food and beverages went out the window, with new arrivals carting in coolers of beer, liquor and all sorts of party supplies. Pot smoke wafted through the air, while people held up signs looking for acid and psychedelic mushrooms. By Saturday, the news reported that Woodstock was once again a "free concert." Those on the grounds were both stunned and stimulated by the gigantic crowd, and while everybody dug the endless hours of music, it was the fact that Woodstock '94 was the wildest scene just about anyone had ever seen that made it exciting.

The music, in fact, revealed the greatest differences between the two Woodstocks. In 1969, the bill reflected a consensus born of the fact that most hippies had the same record collections. In 1994, musical tastes are far more divergent, and while the promoters of Woodstock '94 were aiming at the rock n' roll mainstream with a nod towards hip tastemakers, that still guaranteed a wildly eclectic show. In general, today's bands are also much more professional than those of the late '60s, with concert performances honed by arena tours and codified by the images projected in rock videos. With state-of-the-art sound systems pumping out the thunderous roar on two different stages, and huge video screens affording close-up views of the performers, Woodstock '94 also underscored the huge advances in concert production that have been made in the past twenty-five years.

Shuttling between the two stages – not an easy proposition as the crowd swelled to more than 350,000 – listeners were exposed to a Cliff Notes survey of modern rock. A mix of punk and funk was heard in the music of the Red Hot Chili Peppers and Primus. The cranberries and James offered variations on the moody melodicism of Celtic rock. Sheryl Crow and Melissa Etheridge represented singer-songwriters, with Etheridge paying special tribute to a hero from the first festival, Janis Joplin. Three strains of rap were served: sexy rap (Salt N' Pepa), inspirational rap (Arrested Development) and stoner rap (Cypress Hill). You could trace a trail from the African polyrhythms of Youssou N'Dour to the second-line beats favored by The Neville Brothers of New Orleans, and could also hear the affinity between Santana's Latin rhythms and Jimmy Cliff's Jamaican reggae. Solid sets by veteran groups like the Allman Brothers Band and Traffic showcased the stylistic roots of younger bands like Blues Traveler and the Spin Doctors.

While some acts were content to present their standard concert sets before the biggest audience of their career, others seized the moment. The twisted industrial-rock band Nine Inch Nails got the festival's best laugh by appearing onstage after bathing in mud. When rain pounded the stage during a typically aggressive set by the Rollins Band, singer Henry Rollins shook his fist at the sky, as if challenging Nature's fury with his own. Both bands inspired a frenzy in the mosh pit, a post-modern addition to the Woodstock landscape. In 1969, hippies choreographed solitary, free-form dances. In 1994, people slam-danced in the mosh pit and body-surfed above the crowd until they were slipped back into the mud.

The mosh pit was born of punk rock, and it was during a Sunday afternoon performance by Green Day that the mud met the stage. Inspired by the group's punky songs, the audience began pelting each other with gooey divots of straw. Then, challenged by the trio's verbal taunts that they were nothing but a bunch of "muddy hippies," the crowd began taking aim at the performers. Singer Billie Joe Armstrong abandoned his guitar to return fire. When the stage was overrun with Mud People, bassist Mike Dirnt was so soiled that he was mistaken for an audience member and tackled by security.

Music is what drew everybody to Winston Farm, but that's not what they're likely to remember. Mud is what they'll remember – thick, pungent, oozing mud capable of sucking the shoes right off your feet. After heavy rains on Saturday afternoon, which continued intermittently into Sunday morning, negotiating Winston Farm was to be one slip away from joining the Mud People. By the time Metallica had acres of people punching the air with their fists, the party felt like a cross between spring break and a refugee camp. When Aerosmith finally closed out a hard-rocking Saturday night at 3:30 am, many were already streaming towards the exits – even as thousands more illuminated the field with encore lights.

In the months before Woodstock '94, baby-boom pundits complained that an expensive, corporate-sponsored rock festival commemorating the counter-culture's coming out party was somehow sacrilegious. These arguments ignored the fact that rock n' roll has always been as much about commerce as music, and that the original festival was certainly meant to make money. The truth is that in 1969, the business of rock n' roll was barely out of its infancy; these days popular music is a multibillion dollar enterprise guided by all manner of marketing expertise. In 1969, Woodstock was an event that caught the mainstream by surprise. In 1994, Woodstock was the mainstream, with MTV broadcasting from the site, and a world-wide television audience at home. This time it was not just a rock festival; it was an electronic global village that also resulted in a record, a movie, and this book.

Bob Dylan and Peter Gabriel highlighted the final hours of the weekend. Dylan performed a set consisting mostly of songs old enough to be sung at the original festival; during "I Shall Be Released," a solitary Mud Person surfed over waves of arms reaching up from the mosh pit. Peter Gabriel's music, a savvy blend of art-rock attitudes and world-beat rhythms, demonstrated the sophistication that has distinguished certain styles of rock in the years since the original Woodstock. The message was that where rock n' roll was once seen as music that spoke only to the young, it now reaches far beyond a single generation. Gabriel closed Woodstock '94 on a tranquil note with "Biko," a song about Stephen Biko, the solitary South African martyr. It was a far cry from Jimi Hendrix's incendiary "Star-Spangled Banner" but an appropriate benediction for a weekend billed as "2 more days of peace and music." And as the crowd carefully picked their way out of the sodden site, stars peeked through the clearing sky.

By the time the last guitar chord had sounded in Saugerties, vendors were already selling T-shirts that said, "I Survived Woodstock '94." Survived with grace is more like it, for the salient fact is that more than a third of a million people had spent a weekend partying in a potentially dangerous, thoroughly overtaxed environment with virtually no incidents of violence. In 1994, as in 1969, that spoke volumes about the power of music and

day

11 00	REKK & ROGUISH ARMAMENT
11 35	MASTER OF NONE
12 00 noon	THREE
12 25	FUTU FUTU
12 50	ABBA RAGE
01 15	LUNCH MEAT
01 40	PAUL LUKE BAND
02 05	PEACE BOMB
02 30	GOAT
03 00	ORLEANS
03 40	BLUES TRAVELER
04 30	JACKYL
05 20	DEL AMITRI
06 10	LIVE
07 00	JAMES
07 50	KING'S X
08 40	SHERYL CROW
09 30	COLLECTIVE SOUL
10 20	CANDLEBOX
11 15	VIOLENT FEMMES
02 00 am	RAVESTOCK featuring ORBIT

Christopher John Farley >>> I wasn't looking forward to going back. >>>

To quote Al Pacino in "Godfather III:" "Just when I thought I was out, they pull me back in." I believed,
mistakenly as it turns out, that I had left Woodstock '94 behind me, that the mud, the marketing,
the dirt fights between the punk band Green Day and mosh-pit wackos was all just a memory,
and I was safely back in my bed in Kansas with my Aunty Em standing protectively over me
(metaphorically speaking, of course). Anyways, I thought Woodstock was only a memory.
But it turns out that's the point. Everyone who went to Woodstock, all of us who w

were there, we all have these memories, these stories, and for the rest of our lives we can tell them over and over again, tell them to friend

woodstock.29.1b: wendy & sheryl (WELLy) Fri 12 Aug 94 15:32 Hey Michael & Bob! We're here...camped in the meadow camping area behind south stage, across the footbridge and to the left down at the bottom of the field (flat area) past the Union Jack flagpole...near water and Port-O-Sans.. Where are you? We'll be at the bottom of the footbridge from 8pm-8:30pm Friday... and again 11 - 11:30 Saturday morning. Hope to see you soon! PEACE & LOVE!

who were too cheap and stupid not to buy Woodstock tickets of their own (or too timid to crash the gates), and alternately enthrall and bore

Or

3

future generations of children and grandchildren and stepchildren and test-tube babies who all better damn well listen to us or we'll cut off

3:00 PM

eans

their child support or their inheritance or smash their test tubes or whatever it takes to make them listen to our tales of Woodstock '94.

(W) woodstock.15.55: Dan Levy (WELL) Fri 12 Aug 94 21:03

My favorite Woodstock statement so far came from the stage. John Popper, Blues Traveler's singer and harp man, warned the crowd to watch out for the brown Pepsi, which is not specifically too good.

traveler

> > > That being said, I was actually looking forward to the first day of the concert. The buildup had been enormous. Vendors reportedly

dogs, 125,000 pounds of french fries, 31,250 gallons of coffee and about 2,234,885 quarts of anticipation.

Woodstock was also the talk of cyberspace. "The way I look at it is like this," said one 22-year-old Maryland graduate student in a messag

Nick Ripple Cichanowski (WELL) Fri 12 Aug 94 15:57 Some guy just dropped his drawers onstage and the cameraman felt it necessary to get a close up of his hairy ass...

sent via the Internet, "You get to see some good classic rock (Dylan, Cocker, Aerosmith), the best of the Lollapaloozas (Red Hot Chili

Peppers, Porno for Pyros, Nine Inch Nails), some new upcoming talent (Live, James, Candlebox) and some of the greatest performer

Del Amitri

(Gabriel) all in one sitting! The other Woodstock never had it this good." > > > Of course, good things come to those who wait. The big acts were

Live (from left): Patrick Dahlheimer, Chad Gracey, Chad Taylor, Edward Kowalczyk

scheduled to play later in the weekend. That first day, the roster was filled with local bands and up-and-coming bands and bands that co

Live

a video played on MTV, VH1, CNN, CNBC, KABC, C-SPAN or the Home Shopping Network for that matter. There were Futu Futu and Lunch

W woodstock.13.13: pacifism (WELLS) Fri 12 Aug 94 18:48
People relate to their past through their memories; Woodstock
is the memory of goodwill for everybody, every human being
who's got the right to live and express themselves would enjoy
this event. Two thumbs up for the organizers and artists.

James (from left): Jim Glennie, Tim Booth, Mark Hunter, Larry Gott, David Baynton-Power, Saul Davies

Meat and Huffamoose and — you get the point. Most ordinary lunch-pail-carrying, "New York Times"-reading, "Home Improvement"-wat

1g, cubic zirconium-buying Americans had no idea who these bands were. Even cool people, the ones that started buying Green Day's albums

when they were on tiny Lookout! Records, and who were into Henry Rollins way back when he was with Black Flag – even they had no clu‹

(W) woodstock.23.15: edmon (WELL) Fri 12 Aug 94 19:07
Once there were two monks arguing about a flag. The first said,
"The flag is moving." The second replied, "The wind is moving."
Just then the third patriarch happened to walk by. He said,
"Not the flag, not the wind - the mind is moving."

to put out musically. Sure, the Red Hot Chili Peppers are cool guys, but regardless of whether Anthony Kiedis breaks a sweat on stage or not,

women are going to throw him their panties, and a few of the more liberated guys might well throw him their panties, too. People aren't going

to throw their panties at Huffamoose unless they want them laundered. Woodstock '94 was a huge shot for these opening-day acts. If a small

woodstock·29·2b: debbie of vogue (WELLS) Fri 12 Aug 94 19:33
ATTENTION!!GAIL GOLDBERG AND ALYSSA LUSTIGMAN AND STEPHANIE WILLIAMS,
MY TENT IS ACROSS FROM THE HARLEY DAVIDSON STORE IN THE CRAFT AREA. IF
YOU GET THIS MESSAGE, MEET ME AT THE STORE AT NOON. OTHERWISE, LEAVE A
MESSAGE FOR ME HERE. THIS THING IS HUGE!!!!!!!!!!!!!!!

KinG

time act like Lunch Meat did well at Woodstock, who knows? The next day they could be in heavy rotation on MTV and close personal friends

8:40 PM 42

W woodstock.23.5: (ernie) Fri 12 Aug 94 11:51
In an infinite universe, everything is possible.

sheryl crow

with Tabitha Soren, comparing tattoos with Drew Barrymore and getting into male-bonding bar fights with Mickey Rourke. > > >

There were some newer acts that performed that first night, like Jackyl and King's X and Sheryl Crow and some others. Jackyl, for their

collective

part, put on a crazed, attention-grabbing performance. Lead singer Jesse James Dupree cut himself onstage with a chainsaw, set things

SOUL

Collective Soul (from left: Dean Roland, Matthew Serletic, Ross Childress, Will Turpin, Ed Roland, Shane Evans

re and generally acted like a cross between Beavis, Butt-head and Charles Manson (and not necessarily in that order). Folkie rocker Sheryl

candle

box

Crow sang her poppy hit "All I Wanna Do," but despite looking every bit the rock star in her slinky, velvety purple top, she seemed a bit ov

11:15 PM

Violent Femmes

vhelmed emotionally. But hey, everybody was that first day. Here we all were, having Woodstock all over again; we were back in the garden

0 48500 00137 0

RavE-StOCK 94

(okay, a soon-to-be-muddy field) and back on Max Yasgur's farm (well, a few miles away from it), we were half a million strong (actually

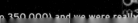

...oser to 350,000) and we were really doing it — we were having our own Woodstock! Screw the baby boomers! You got Richie Havens — we g...

Q: Where were you at the last Woodstock?

Lady Miss Kier: I'll never forget the first time I heard the "Star-Spangled Banner" on the radio. My mom had painted our house black and we had American flags for curtains and she had giant daisies painted on the house. The house was really overgrown and we were like the freaks of the neighborhood. When I heard that on the radio I knew there was a whole lot of people just like us.

missKier

baby boomers had a slight edge on the musical scorecard, but then again they got Vietnam and we got no wars at all really, except for that thing

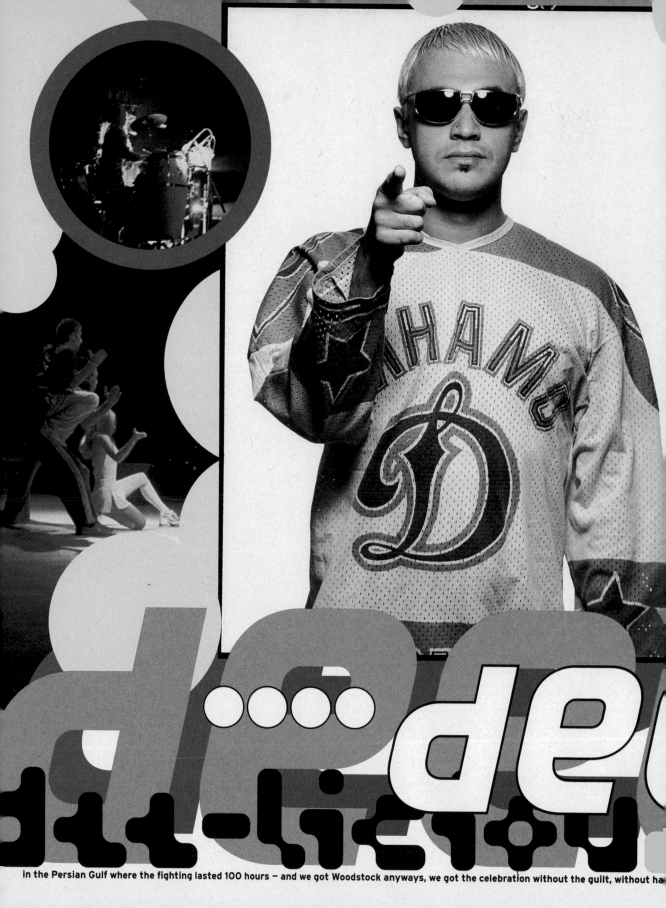

in the Persian Gulf where the fighting lasted 100 hours — and we got Woodstock anyways, we got the celebration without the guilt, without ha

woodstock·13.25: on the other side of the sun (miga) Sat 13 Aug 94 11:37 Oh, Erinita, I was looking for you! You missed the Orb, I'm afraid..they went on at about 4:15 am after a shortish Aphex Twin set...The Orb was just absolutely stellar. They did more dance beats than usual and blended familiar samples/themes from their tracks with new beats and samples...there was an incredible tribal break! But I'm getting ahead of myself. At about 4:30 or so lightning began to flash in the sky, and it misted a little. I was saying, "No rain! No rain!" but a bit later it started to rain—big drops—and I thought I'd surely catch cold but NO WAY was I going to leave until they stopped playing! The rain went on just long enough for the fainthearted to take off, then miraculously stopped! They went on till nearly 7:30 and it was great...The Orb was just outstanding, and the crowd at the end was definitely a typical early-morning rave scene, people dancing and smiling. Yeah!

pe-lite

...ng to burn draft cards or fake chronic ailments to escape military duty. We got Woodstock anyways. The first day was over and we were loving

SOULSLINGER

LIQUID SKY

it. Screw the baby boomers (except, of course, for the ones in attendance). Woodstock — and rock n' roll itself — was our trip now.

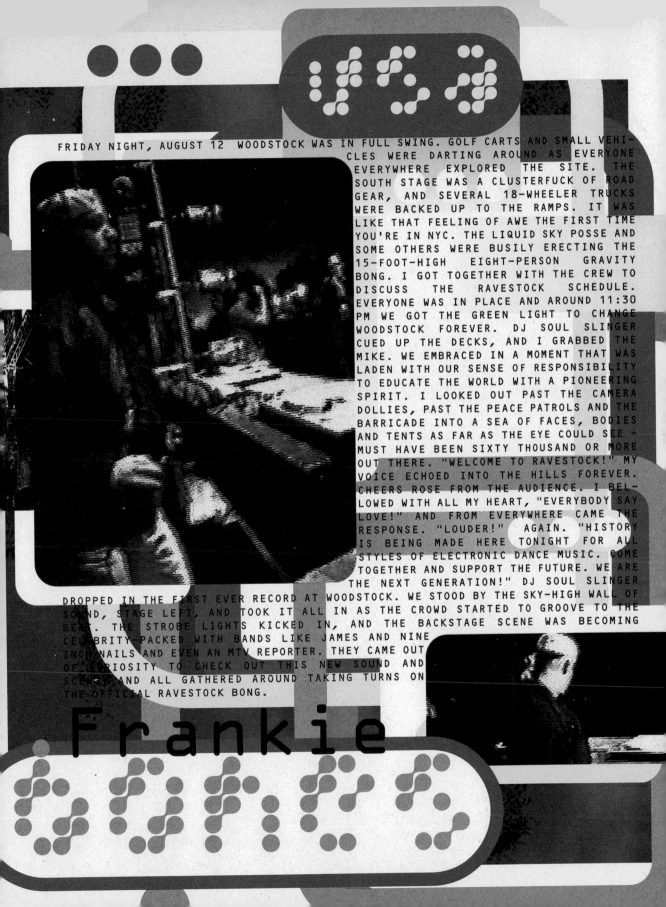

FRIDAY NIGHT, AUGUST 12 WOODSTOCK WAS IN FULL SWING. GOLF CARTS AND SMALL VEHI-CLES WERE DARTING AROUND AS EVERYONE EVERYWHERE EXPLORED THE SITE. THE SOUTH STAGE WAS A CLUSTERFUCK OF ROAD GEAR, AND SEVERAL 18-WHEELER TRUCKS WERE BACKED UP TO THE RAMPS. IT WAS LIKE THAT FEELING OF AWE THE FIRST TIME YOU'RE IN NYC. THE LIQUID SKY POSSE AND SOME OTHERS WERE BUSILY ERECTING THE 15-FOOT-HIGH EIGHT-PERSON GRAVITY BONG. I GOT TOGETHER WITH THE CREW TO DISCUSS THE RAVESTOCK SCHEDULE. EVERYONE WAS IN PLACE AND AROUND 11:30 PM WE GOT THE GREEN LIGHT TO CHANGE WOODSTOCK FOREVER. DJ SOUL SLINGER CUED UP THE DECKS, AND I GRABBED THE MIKE. WE EMBRACED IN A MOMENT THAT WAS LADEN WITH OUR SENSE OF RESPONSIBILITY TO EDUCATE THE WORLD WITH A PIONEERING SPIRIT. I LOOKED OUT PAST THE CAMERA DOLLIES, PAST THE PEACE PATROLS AND THE BARRICADE INTO A SEA OF FACES, BODIES AND TENTS AS FAR AS THE EYE COULD SEE — MUST HAVE BEEN SIXTY THOUSAND OR MORE OUT THERE. "WELCOME TO RAVESTOCK!" MY VOICE ECHOED INTO THE HILLS FOREVER. CHEERS ROSE FROM THE AUDIENCE. I BEL-LOWED WITH ALL MY HEART, "EVERYBODY SAY LOVE!" AND FROM EVERYWHERE CAME THE RESPONSE. "LOUDER!" AGAIN. "HISTORY IS BEING MADE HERE TONIGHT FOR ALL STYLES OF ELECTRONIC DANCE MUSIC. COME TOGETHER AND SUPPORT THE FUTURE. WE ARE THE NEXT GENERATION!" DJ SOUL SLINGER DROPPED IN THE FIRST EVER RECORD AT WOODSTOCK. WE STOOD BY THE SKY-HIGH WALL OF SOUND, STAGE LEFT, AND TOOK IT ALL IN AS THE CROWD STARTED TO GROOVE TO THE BEAT. THE STROBE LIGHTS KICKED IN, AND THE BACKSTAGE SCENE WAS BECOMING CELEBRITY-PACKED WITH BANDS LIKE JAMES AND NINE INCH NAILS AND EVEN AN MTV REPORTER. THEY CAME OUT OF CURIOSITY TO CHECK OUT THIS NEW SOUND AND SCENE, AND ALL GATHERED AROUND TAKING TURNS ON THE OFFICIAL RAVESTOCK BONG.

Frankie

ORBITAL HAD ARRIVED FROM ENGLAND AT THE LAST MINUTE, AND WE SWAPPED THE SCHEDULE AROUND TO ACCOMMODATE THEIR NEEDS. THEY SET UP, PERFORMED, PACKED UP THE GEAR AND JUMPED ON A CONCORDE AT 6:00 AM TO PERFORM AGAIN IN THE SOUTH OF FRANCE. TWO NIGHTS BEFORE, ORBITAL HAD PLAYED A FESTIVAL IN AMSTERDAM. TALK ABOUT FREQUENT-FLYER MILES. THEIR MULTI-MEDIA PERFORMANCE MESMERIZED THE AUDIENCE AS THE ELECTRONIC SUB-BASS ROCKED THROUGH THE FIELDS. THEIR POLITICALLY INSPIRED VIDEO SUMMED UP OUR COLLECTIVE VIBE IN THAT OUR ILL-TREATMENT OF THE ENVIRONMENT IS DAMAGING US TOO.

THE DEEE-LITE SHOW DEFINITELY COMMANDED THE LARGEST CAPTIVE AUDIENCE. PEOPLE WERE SURFING THE CROWD AND STAGE DIVING BY THE THIRD SONG. AND THERE WAS NO ESCAPING RICHARD JAMES, A.K.A. APHEX TWIN. HE WALKED ONSTAGE, SEGUED INTO THE NIGHT AND PLAYED HARD AS FUCK, LOBBING SONIC GRENADES INTO THROBBING EARS. MY FELLOW APHEX FAN DAVE PRINCE AND I HAD A SUDDEN PAGAN INSPIRATION. WE STRIPPED DOWN NAKED AND DANCED OUR ASSES OFF NEAR THE STAGE'S LEFT WING! PEOPLE WERE CHEER-ING, SWEATING, WITH HANDS IN THE AIR AND WHISTLES BLOWING. THE ULTIMATE RAVE AT ITS HARDEST PEAK UNDER THE STARS. BUT THE MOST INSPIRATIONAL PART CAME WHEN THE ENGLISH GROUP THE ORB CAME ON FOR AN UNFORGETTABLE EVENING. THEY TOOK US (AND THOSE SLEEPING INSIDE TENTS) ON A DREAMY JOURNEY INTO THE GLOW OF THE MORNING SUNRISE.

SUNDAY NIGHT, AUGUST 14 NEAR THE END OF PETER GABRIEL'S SHOW AT THE NORTH STAGE, ONE OF THE PIONEERS OF DETROIT TECHNO TOOK TO THE SOUTH STAGE TO KICK OFF RAVESTOCK, PART TWO. FROM THE STAGE TO THE MIX TOWER, MUD WAS AT LEAST A FOOT DEEP. SLOWLY A CROWD GATHERED, READY FOR ANYTHING EXCEPT MORE RAIN. THEN, AT ABOUT 1:00 AM MONDAY MORNING, THE ORB'S MEGA-LIGHT-NING STROBES SET OFF NATURE'S THUNDER. RAVERS TOOK SHELTER FROM THE LAST WOODSTOCK RAIN AS THE ORB TURNED UP THE MASSIVE SOUND SYSTEM AND THE ROAR OF A MOTORCYCLE FILLED THE TOWN NOW OVERRUN WITH PEOPLE LEAVING SAUGERTIES. TIRED, MUDDY AND WORN-OUT PEOPLE TURNED BACK AND CHEERED. CANDLES, BROUGHT OVER FROM GABRIEL'S SHOW, WERE RE-LIT AS SEVERAL HUNDRED GATHERED IN A CIRCLE, FORMING A SORT OF PEACE SYMBOL IN FRONT OF THE STAGE. BY THE END OF THE TWO HOUR EXPERIENCE, SEVERAL THOUSAND HAD WANDERED OVER, AND THEY WERE REALLY GROOVIN'.

HOPEFULLY RAVESTOCK MADE PEOPLE AWARE OF OUR PRIMAL NOCTURNAL URGE TO GATHER — TO DANCE, TO EXPRESS OUR ROOTS, LOVE OUR BROTHER AND BE GRATEFUL FOR LIFE! WE ARE GLOBALLY LINKED TOGETHER, UNITED IN OUR PASSION FOR MUSIC. I'LL NEVER FORGET WHEN, DURING HIS SHOW, DJ SOUL SLINGER LOOKED UP AT ME FROM HIS RECORD BOX AND SAID, "YOU'VE GOT TO BELIEVE THAT MUSIC SAVES OUR LIVES!" SO RESPECT, SUPPORT YOUR SCENE AND LET THE FEELING OF SELF-WORTH CARESS YOU.

PEACE,   SCOTTO

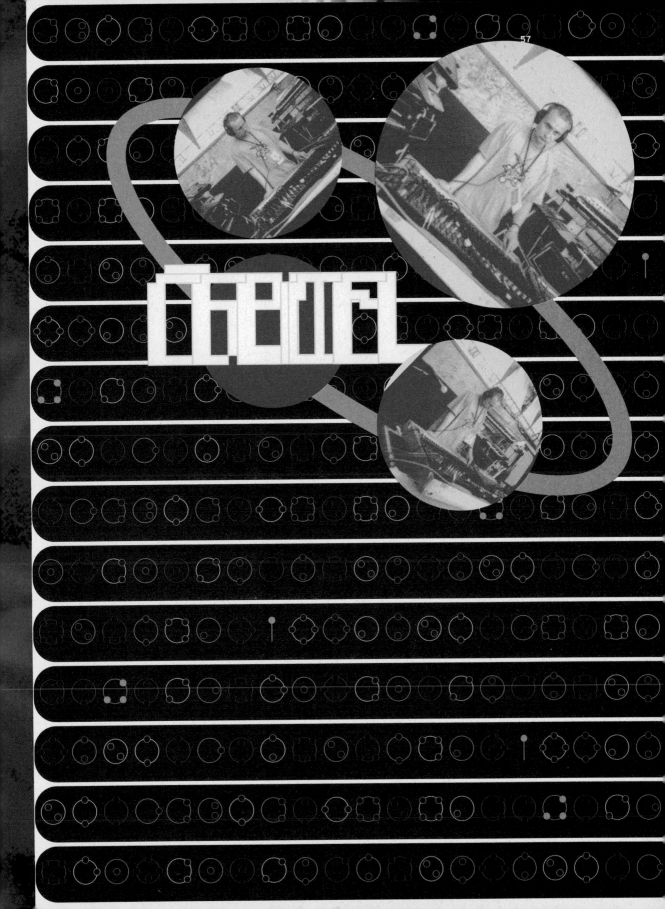

N

JOE COCKER	12 00
BLIND MELON	01 30
CYPRESS HILL	02 45
ROLLINS BAND	03 25
MELISSA ETHERIDGE	05 10
CROSBY, STILLS AND NASH	06 45
NINE INCH NAILS	08 30
METALLICA	10 30
AEROSMITH	12 15

S

12 30	THE CRANBERRIES
01 30	ZUCCHERO
02 30	YOUSSOU N'DOUR
03 45	THE BAND
06 30	PRIMUS
07 45	SALT N' PEPA

The second day. We woke up and we were still at Woodstock. It hadn't been a dream, and we weren't crazy. But what w
se voices in our heads? Public announcements. Throughout the three days, concert organizers would read announcements fr
stage – reminders, warnings, jokes, little things and big things that were meant to give the attendees some
community and reality. "We've got a lot of responsibility. Let's make sure that all these assholes in the press that thir
deserve your own Woodstock are wrong," went one announcement. Another declared: "This from the medical staff:
There is laced marijuana. People are having side effects. So be careful."

No wonder it didn't feel real. Would the promoters really be able to pull this off? Could Aerosmith, th

08:15 A M 60

Metallica, Cypress Hill, Primus and all the other bands who were scheduled to perform that second day really turn this into another

Woodstock, a real Woodstock, a Woodstock we wouldn't be ashamed to tell our friends that we had attended?   >>>   And then Joe Cocker

took the stage. This guy is a rock survivor. He'd been there, done that, seen it all and now he was back at Woodstock. Some of us remem

ered Cocker from the original Woodstock movie, and a lot of Woodstock '94 attendees (myself included) had rented the videocassette to

Joe Cocker was the guy who I was most moved by at Woodstock. I just saw him today, and he's still great. Twenty-five years has not diminished the man's power.

Bruce Hornsby

prepare themselves for this sequel. In the 1969 movie, Cocker was a wild-haired young man with big sideburns, clad in a fashion-defying t

dyed T-shirt, pin-striped pants and star-spangled boots. And here he was again in the flesh. 1994. He was older now, and he certainly was a

the cranberries (from left): Fergal Lawler, Dolores O'Riordan, Noel Hogan, Mike Hogan

better dresser than he was in '69 – nothing he was wearing now was pin-striped, tie-dyed or star-spangled (though I can't and won't vouc

the cranberries

for his undies). Also gone were his huge, hairy sideburns (I think they're on loan to Neil Young). But one thing was for sure – he could still

Glen Graham

Brad Smith

sing up a storm. He had a voice like a weather front moving in, full of dark clouds and thunder. Cocker sang "You Are So Beautiful" and "Cry

Rogers Stevens

Shannon Hoon

Christopher Thor

Me A River," and his near-flawless performance showed off the wisdom and skill of a veteran. But when Cocker ripped into his cover of the

Woodstock 17/28: Danica Remy (WELL3) Sat 13 Aug
09:33 Hey, live over the walkie talkie on my
belt. Two hundred people have pushed the fence over
that goes into the VIP backstage area. The concert
promoters have six guys at the fence now. Good
luck six guys with hundreds walking through. Walkie
talkie report says fence reinforcers on their way.
Hope they know the back way...

BLIND

Beatles' "With A Little Help From My Friends," with that tender, heartfelt beginning "What would you do if I sang out of tune?" – it was then

that we were all finally certain this wasn't a dream. This was Woodstock all over again, only this time we had plenty of Port-O-Sans. Cocker

ZUCCHERO

finished with a flourish, saying, "See you again in 2019." Actually, I'm booked that weekend, but given the endurance that man has

73

02:30 PM

Youssou N'Dour

hown over the decades, I'm sure I'll catch him again in 2044. > > > Blind Melon was next, and lead singer Shannon Hoon got caught up in

Cypress Hill (from left): DJ Muggs, B-Real, BoBo, Sen-Dog

the momentousness of the whole occasion. He wanted to do something wild, something outrageous, something that would sy

cypress hill

ustration of his entire overhyped, overmarketed, underemployed and underwhelmed twentysomething generation. So he wore a shabby

white dress and removed his underwear onstage (I can vouch that his undergarments were not star-spangled). Hoon sang some of his songs

...d screamed others ("I got this fucked-up view from all of you!"), mascara smeared around his eyes, stubble on his face, girly-man...

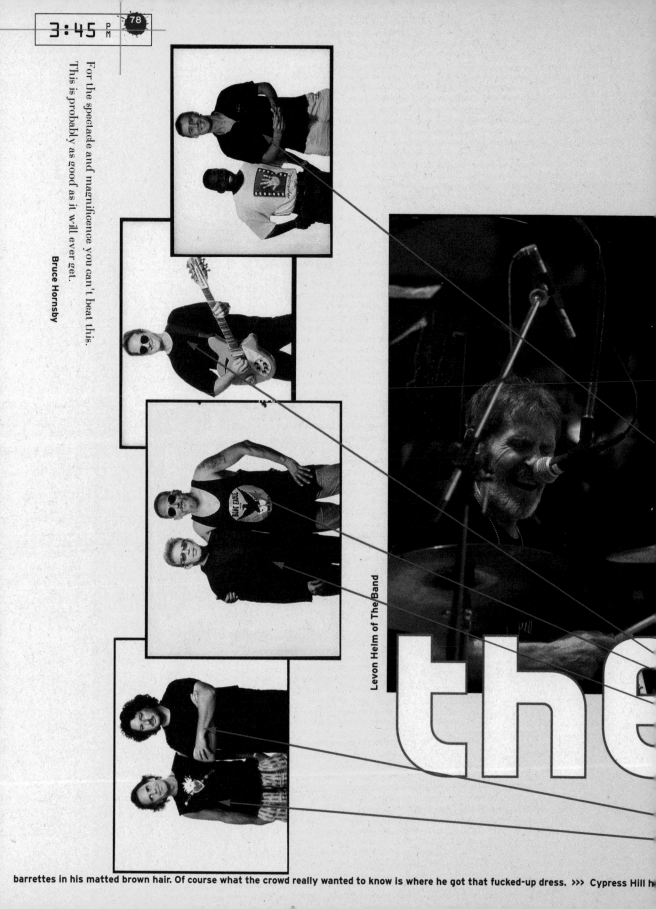

For the spectacle and magnificence you can't beat this. This is probably as good as it will ever get.

Bruce Hornsby

Levon Helm of The Band

the

barrettes in his matted brown hair. Of course what the crowd really wanted to know is where he got that fucked-up dress. >>> Cypress Hill h

Garth Hudson of The Band

Band

THE BAND'S BIG PINK REVIEW

featuring performances by

Bob Weir & Rob Wasserman, Roger McGuinn, Hot Tuna & Bruce Hornsby

he stage looking to make trouble. The Los Angeles rap trio brought a model of a huge hand holding a joint onto the stage. Lead rapper B-Real

suilloR

band

Rollins Band (from left): Chris Haskett, Sim Cain, Melvin Gibbs, Theo Van Rock, Henry Rollins

fired up a blunt. "I'm taking a hit for every one of y'all," he said magnanimously, though he wasn't charitable enough to pass whatever it was h

s smoking to the fans in the first row.   > > >   You could tell that B-Real was intensely aware of his audience, of the size and sweep of the

When the wind blew towards the stage all you could smell was the sweat of over three hundred and fifty thousand people. It was so much flesh, humans as far as you could see,

crowd. He kept looking out into the crowd, drinking in the reality that this was the biggest crowd they had ever played in front of, that there w

Time seemed to hang suspended while we played. While I was walking off, I tried to look out there so hard that I would never forget it. We had a blast.

Henry Rollins

Generation X," he snarled. "I say we're Generation Fuck You." It didn't quite have the ring of Gertrude Stein's "The Lost Generation," but it wa

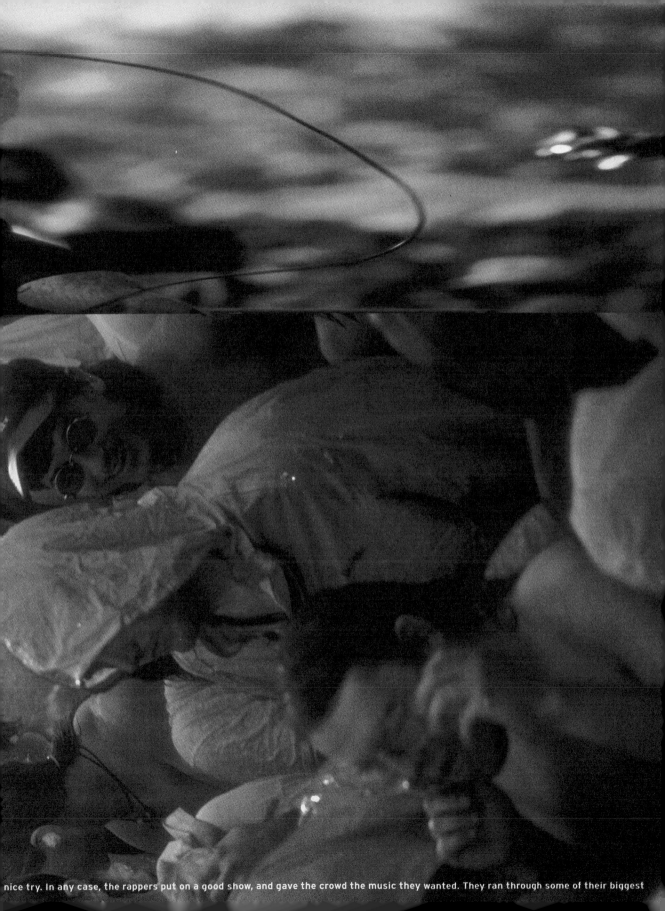

nice try. In any case, the rappers put on a good show, and gave the crowd the music they wanted. They ran through some of their biggest

(W) woodstock.31.14: cerise (WELL4) Sat 13 Aug 94 14:46
Just got back from the south stage where The Band was just about t
when the skies opened up. The equipment, the instruments, the art
the crowd got drenched!
Wavy Gravy carried on with a MORE RAIN cheer--the crowd loved it!
The rain finally stopped, leaving behind a field full of mud, and
The Band went on...

songs, such as "Insane In The Brain" and "I Ain't Goin' Out Like That." During that last song, B-Real threw himself into the crowd and body-sur

He wanted to be part of Woodstock, and the crowd was what it was all about. That was how he was going out. Henry Rollins

and the Rollins Band took the stage next. Within seconds, it seemed, Rollins was shirtless, his tattoos exposed for all to see, flexing his pecs, ab

Melissa Etheridge

Woodstock was an incredible experience for me. I had no idea what it would be like playing at such an enormous event. On arriving at the concert site I walked out into the crowd to watch Joe Cocker. When he went into "A Little Help From My Friends," I was carried away. The combination of being part of an audience of 350,000 people and experiencing Joe Cocker was exhilarating.

Then it was my turn to perform. Words alone cannot describe my feelings and emotions as I stepped onto the stage. As I looked out over the crowd that stretched to the horizon, I had to fight to control myself. My energy level was so high I felt as if I could fly from the stage. During my set I included a tribute to Janis Joplin. I wanted to acknowledge how she influenced my music and to somehow bridge the twenty-five years between the two Woodstocks.

I hope I'm invited back to perform at Woodstock III twenty-five years from now.

...and a variety of other muscle groups on his body, attacking each song he performed like it had stolen something from him. When he did "Liar," the

mosh pit went wild. Vitality was pouring off him like hot sweat. "I'm 33," Rollins growled. "I want to live till I'm 100." Throughout the set, th

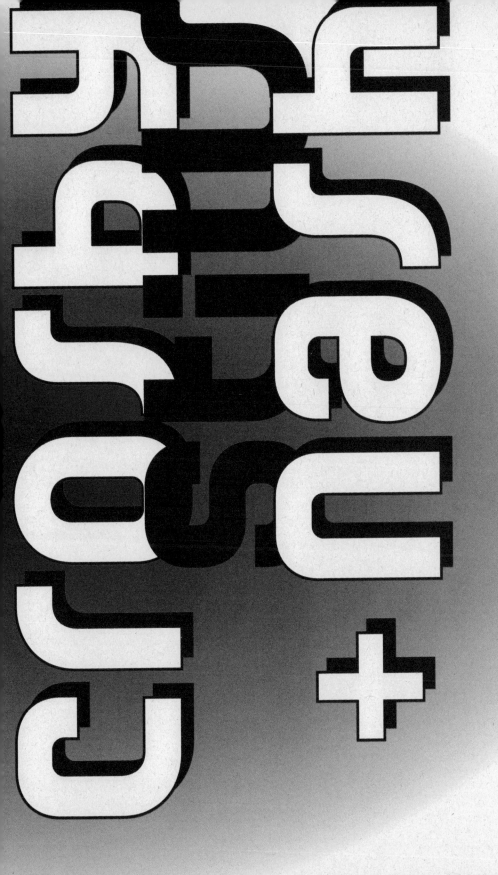

eavy rain started and stopped and started and it almost seemed to be keeping time with what was happening onstage,

adding to the dynamics of Rollins' earnest, musclebound performance. That afternoon you didn't have to be into his music to tap into his energy

he clouds above us join and separate,
he breeze in the courtyard leaves and
eturns. Life is like that, so why not relax?
ho can stop us from celebrating?
                    Lu Yu, Chinese poet and philosopher

was an animal, crouching low, barking his lyrics at the crowd. Only this animal was unleashed, untrained and definitely unspayed. It was in all

6:50 PM

woodstock.15.72: MIvler (WELL2) Sat 13 Aug 94 13:41
I am having a great time here. The rain
but we all got wet and we partied on

ally hit you how much there was to watch. Beyond the op-ed whining about heavy security, miles of fences and drug-sniffing police dogs (if

woodstock 15.78: Jagerer (WELL3) Sun 14 Aug 94 14:37

Besides, it's cool to see
rich people covered in MU

Lisa, you're right

Hope you are feeling

those canines were really all that great, how did Cypress Hill get in?), Woodstock was a Lollapalooza of a concert, times ten and then some. >

. . .I'm sitting in the mud with a
black trash bag as my grounder, hap-
pier than most 'cause I realize what
a joke--I may have mud on my hands,
my face, my feet, but at least not
on my ass!

!!!

ould play hard to get.

od and muddy right now.

e north stage wasn't the only place where things were happening. There was a whole village of vending booths. Need your ear pierced? Seven

bucks. Nose? Ten bucks. Tongue? Negotiable, probably, though I didn't ask. There was also plenty of food for sale, though it should be pointed o

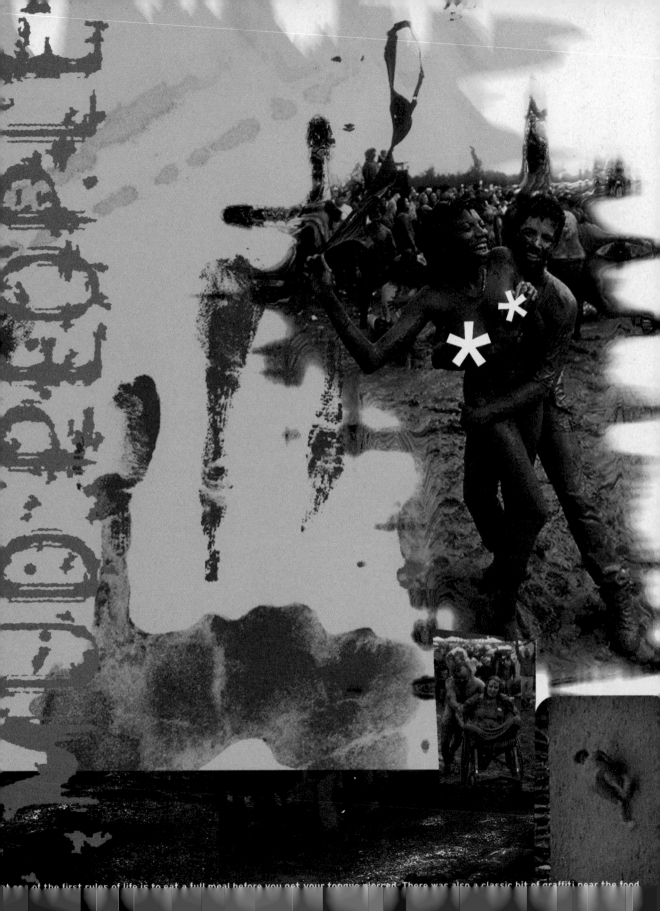

Yeah I was there, 17 in
Mostly I remember the
around dusk and most of
when you entered
it was similar to enterin
to throw off your sens
smoking opium with a sna
covered in mud b
the peac

booths: "Woodstock II: Where the munchies cost more than the drugs." Hey, just say no to snack food, dude.   >>>   There was also plenty

went early to make sure I could get in.
n Crosby, Stills and Nash were playing
ldings were kinda tilting in the mud so
tance an abandoned "liberated" food stand
m in a fun house that has been tilted on end
vity and in one corner would be a dude
pped around his or someone head to toe
ked...the press always makes a big deal of
v aspect and the mud....

ctivity on the south stage. Over there, the dreamy Irish band the cranberries were charming the crowd; they were followed by Sen

PRI
MU
S

songsmith Youssou N'Dour and then by Salt N' Pepa, who put on a show that was half aerobics workout, half rap, and half Sex Ed 101. Sure, th

Primus (from left): Tim "Herb" Alexander, Les Claypool, Larry Lalonde

Etheridge – her big rough voice, her oversized power chords. Ever since she proudly declared to the world that she was gay, her music to me ha

epa

seemed more bouncy and exuberant than ever. She leapt feet-first into her joyous top-40 rocker "Come To My Window,"

Q: What was it like performing for a crowd celebrating the anniversary of Woodstock?

Sandra Denton ('Pepa'): They knew who Salt N' Pepa was. They were waiting for Salt N' Pepa. And I'd do it again. Now, rap has gotten so large that everyone knows what rap is.

next two acts on the north stage couldn't have been more different: Crosby, Stills and Nash and industrial noise-freaks

NINE INCH NAILS

Nine Inch Nails. > > >   Like Cocker, Crosby, Stills and Nash brought with them a sense of history. Their haunting, lovely rendering of "Suite

just take the picture so
we can get the fuck out
of here.
    Robin Finck

ragged, but there they were. "Southern Cross" was the best number they did. It wasn't just their voices, gliding up and down the gorgeou

woodstock.67.21: well's cargo (dlee)   Thu 18 Aug 94 11:08

One of the images that sticks to me most relentlessly is of NIN. When they came out onstage looking straight from the mudpits and launched into their screaming, powerful onslaught, it was a hell of a thing. Getting down and dirty all the way, no holds barred. I don't know what to think of them, but they definitely got it goin' on.

aves of the song, it was also the gentle orange light of the sunset. The day wasn't just drawing to a close, an era was. Crosby, Stills and Nash

Q: From what you've seen so far, what does the Woodstock anniversary mean to you and the crowd?

Lars Ulrich: It's about creating a festival and putting an event together that means something to the people of 1994. If they want to call it 'Woodstock Two' or 'Saugerties Seven'... I don't think that really makes a difference.

met

and all the other rockers of the '60s era were sailing into the sunset, like King Arthur being ferried away by the Lady of the Lake. But now

T

ca

themselves in mud and were slam-dancing. It was Bacchanalian, it was Dionysian, and it was hard to remember that this was all real, and not

just a fantasy. Reznor saw what was going on and wanted to be part of it, wanted to take it all in and send it back out in the form of rock. He and

Aerosmith (from left): Joe Perry, Steven Tyler, Brad Whitford, Joey Kramer, Tom Hamilton

his band coated themselves in mud before they took the stage. On TV it looked scary, repulsive – exactly what he probably was aiming for. This

ero

sings about feeling like he is made of clay and voices his fear that no one else has ever felt similarly. Not that night, not that Saturday. There

It poured like a cow pissing on a flat rock. Summer thunderstorm in a Catskill cattle pasture with 350,000 Mud People standing in it. Aerosmith was supposed to play at midnight, but midnight came and went. We got the word to go on at 1:15. Time to take the bull by the bag. We formed a circle around Joey's drums and Steven yelled, "WAKE UP, KIDS!" as we began "Eat the Rich." We got our first look at the humongous crowd, lit by the orange glow from the light towers. "Toys in the Attic," "Fever," "F.I.N.E." and "Rag Doll" while the rain came down. Steven, working at the unprotected front of the stage, was wetter than wet. Then we deployed "Cryin'," "Crazy," "Monkey on My Back," "Mama Kin" and "Shut Up and Dance."

Two in the morning, rain stops. Joe Perry takes over and telecasts some blues and "Walk on Down." Next, the four songs that build the climax of our show. The set list taped to the stage floor reads: JANIE, ELEVATOR, DUDE and SWEET E. You fill in the blanks.

Tom starts "Sweet Emotion" with some bass guitar. Brad's rhythm guitar is an emergency telegram. During fifteen months of touring GET A GRIP around the planet, we'd been playing some old Zeppelin licks near the end of our set. At Woodstock this went off like a grenade. The huge crowd exploded as we walked off and didn't stop until the encores. At Woodstock we added John Lennon's "Come Together" to "Dream On" (we saw a hundred thousand lighters fired up at the opening chords), "Living on the Edge" and "Walk This Way."

At 3:30 on Sunday morning we waved goodnight. Back at the deserted artists' compound, we were nearly blown away by the massive post-concert fireworks launched from the hill above us. Up in the black sky, giant erupting poppies. Explosive novas of red light. Gunpowder blasts of roman candles, louder than bombs. Wild sunflowers of fire a hundred feet above our heads. We took it personally.

Leaving the sleeping city of rock an hour later, someone looked at the thousands of tents clustered on the hillsides like refugees and murmured something about Hutus and Tutsis. The ferry down the dark and empty Hudson River at dawn was like crossing to Avalon. A big watch-fire blazed on the dock at Red Hook. An hour later we rode the western winds home, too tired to speak much that morning, but everyone was psyched. It didn't even seem real. Had Aerosmith closed the show on Saturday night at Woodstock '94?

Dream on. . .   aerosmith

were thousands of other souls caked in the same claylike mud, feeling the same thing.

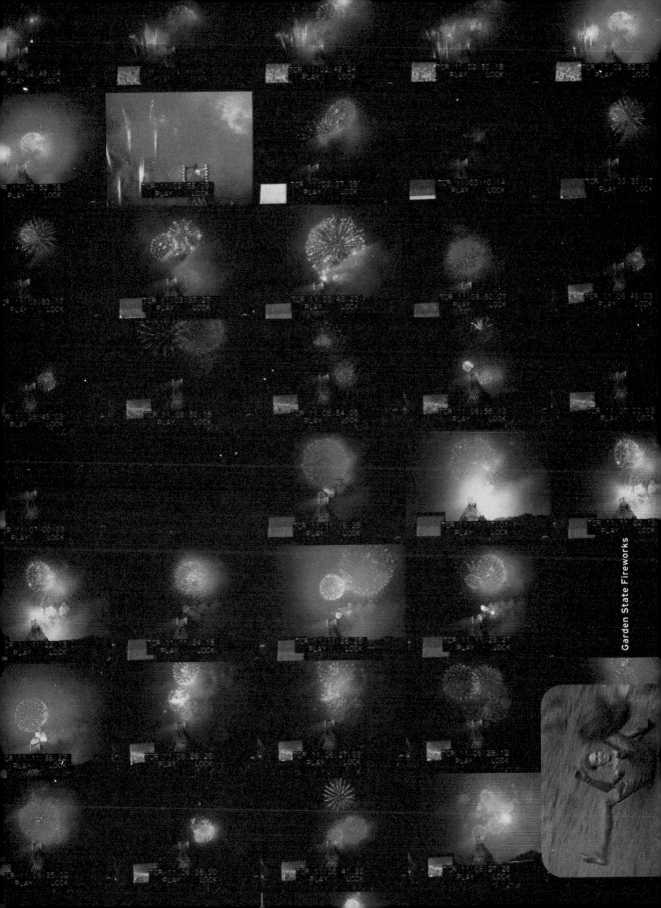

Garden State Fireworks

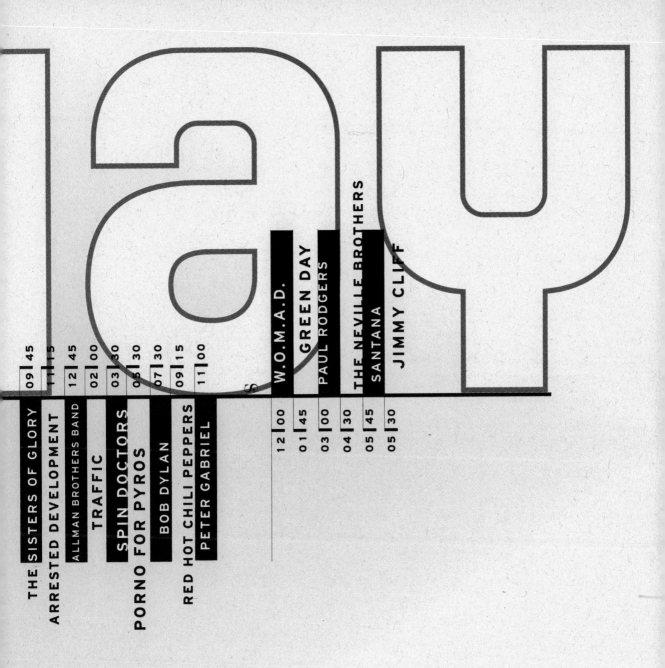

lay Y

09 45	THE SISTERS OF GLORY
11 15	ARRESTED DEVELOPMENT
12 45	ALLMAN BROTHERS BAND
02 00	TRAFFIC
03 30	SPIN DOCTORS
05 30	PORNO FOR PYROS
07 30	BOB DYLAN
09 15	RED HOT CHILI PEPPERS
11 00	PETER GABRIEL
12 00	W.O.M.A.D.
01 45	GREEN DAY
03 00	PAUL RODGERS
04 30	THE NEVILLE BROTHERS
05 45	SANTANA
05 30	JIMMY CLIFF

> > > On day three, the last day, there was "Joy in Mudville." This despite the fact that it had been a long, cold night. Concertgoers had been burning empty Woodstock pizza boxes to keep warm (an announcement later informed us this was a dumb, dangerous idea). Now it was morning. Everyone was ready to rock. Of course, now that the cold night was over, there was the mud to deal with.

Mud, mud, mud. A light rain had been falling on the Woodstock concert grounds all morning and everything was mud. The mud grabbed at your shoes and pulled like tiny insistent hands. The hundreds of multicolored,

New York Times

New Yo
storms,
storms,
morrow,
high 91,

NEW YORK, SUNDAY, AUGUST 14, 1994 $2.50 beyond the greater New York metropolitan area.

Woodstock Redux: New Sea of Young People

200,000 Fans Hear A Musical Medley In Familiar Mud

By JANNY SCOTT
Special to The New York Times

SAUGERTIES, N.Y., Aug. 13 — The 25th-anniversary Woodstock celebration today took on the look of a benign natural disaster attended by more than 200,000 mostly cheerful victims. State officials declared the concert site and its parking areas filled to saturation and began blocking off roads as far as 15 miles away to try to stop more people, including ticket-holders, from coming.

A vast sea of tents and bodies swamped the rolling hills, woods and creek beds of the 840-acre farm where the festival is being held this weekend, making it increasingly difficult to clear away accumulating trash and maneuver emergency vehicles. Rivers of people inching their way toward toilets, telephones, water and food snaked interminably past encampments of tents and groggy, recumbent bodies.

The New York State Police predicted it would take 20 to 25 hours to clear the site after the concert winds down late Sunday because most people will have to be loaded onto school buses and shuttled to parking lots as far as 30 miles away. The task could become complicated by thunderstorms late Sunday afternoon.

Rain was already falling steadily by late this afternoon, and as many as 100 people could be seen dancing to the rap music of Cypress Hill in a large mud lagoon in the main festival field. Elsewhere, people could be found completely covered in mud in

Jose R. Lopez/The New York Times

People dancing in a pit of mud yesterday near the main North stage at

multishaped tents that had been erected were now afloat on a swamp of mud; it looked like a refugee camp. The mud got on your face and your

CRIM
GROW
AN

WEAPO

President
a Pr
Blo

B
Spe

WASHIN
dent Clint
publicans
over the
crime bill
that centra
was defea
cedural vo
tact, while
a major ov

In tense
shape the
in particul
ons ban.

In his
morning, M
no circum
the ban t
legislation.

But with
of Kansas,
Representa
Georgia, th
called for
ences over
not be pe
passage of

At their

rise & shine

ands and there was nowhere to wipe it off except your pants, which were already muddy, and after awhile you just gave

in, you had to give in, to the mud. It's what united the experiences of everyone who went to Woodstock '94. Whether you were young or old, black

r white, straight or gay, a Porno for Pyros fan or a gospel lover who had only come to Woodstock to hear The Sisters of Glory, your feet, your

soul, your life was covered in Woodstock mud.   > > >   The hills at the concert site were slick with it, and some attendees began holding mud

lide races down the slopes, and slip-and-slide foot races back up it. Evidently that didn't prove exciting or dangerous or boneheaded enough,

The Sister

SONGMASTERS INSIDE-OUT presents GOSPEL MUSIC: FROM THE CHURCH TO THE CHARTS starring THE SISTERS OF GLORY, featuring (from left): Phoebe Snow, Thelma Houston, CeCe Peniston, Lois Walden, Mavis Staples

because pretty soon they were holding shopping-cart races – one demented soul sits in the shopping cart, another pushes it, another team doe

the same thing and whoever rolls down the steep mudslick hill first without snapping their spine, wins.

Print File®
ARCHIVAL PRESERVERS

P.O. BOX 607638 · ORLANDO, FL 32860 · (407) 886-3100 .

INSERT EMULSION SIDE DOWN

STYLE NO. 2x2–20B

DATE:

ASSIGNMENT:

FILE NO.:

arrested development

own fledgling community (they more than likely had their own constitution, but it was probably too muddy to read) and

Q: What was it like to play at Woodstock '94?

Headliner: It's a mixture of everything. That's what makes music beautiful, when people can come togeth[er] travel distances just to hear beautiful sounds and mix with one another. • • • •

they moved in packs. Every so often the cry would go up – "Mud People!" – and those of us who still had a few clean spots on our bodies would

That's what makes life more worth living and the music more worth making.

move out of the way as a phalanx of Mud People paraded by, ready and willing to dirty up anyone who impeded their

(W)

woodstock.29.3b: jordanl (WELL2) Sun 14 Aug 94 16:23

OTIS: It's Sunday, where are you?

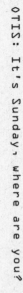

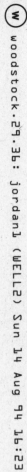

Arrested Development (from left): Headliner, Eshe, Rasa Don, Speech, Ajile, Baba Oje, Nadirah, Kwesi

walked around, unashamed by the attentions of gawkers and television cameras. Women with big breasts and pierced

nipples with rings in them sat on the shoulders of their boyfriends, showing off firm endowments that didn't need the help of Wonderbras to

raw stares. Somewhere, someplace, I figured there was a mother watching pay-per-view, seeing her teenager display her muddy naked bosom

and wondering where her parenting had gone so terribly wrong. > > > This was the last day, this was a happy day and, most important, th

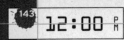

world

of

music

and

dance

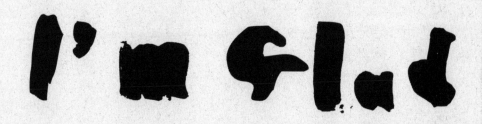

afternoon. However, W.O.M.A.D. – the Peter Gabriel-led World of Music and Dance touring festival that features pop artists from around th

EMCEES

world – was on first, and the crowd grew impatient. "Fucking GREEN DAY," a stocky woman next to me kept demanding, and her bellowing,

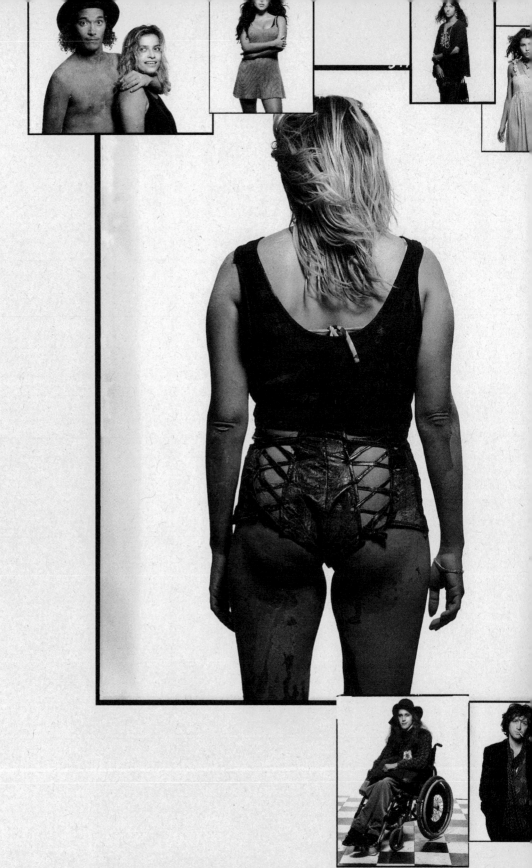

demanding voice was only a decibel or two less than the speakers being used to broadcast the sounds of W.O.M.A.D. "FUCKING Green DAY!"

Faces of Woodstock 2

any case, W.O.M.A.D. was terrific, and the African and Eastern European performers who were associated with it put on gutsy performances in

Allman Brotn

the face of a crowd that was muddy and obsessed with Green Day. At one point Peter Gabriel himself came out and told the crowd to pay atte

Band

on to the world musicians who were performing. For a minute, the entire crowd felt publicly shamed, like Bart Simpson being forced to write his

apologies on the classroom blackboard. Woodstock: Maximum rhythm and blues and lessons in civility, too.   > > >   The crowd had become

thing with a mind of its own, like an ant colony or a flock of birds. Things were being done in unison. Crowd members were having difficulty going

Art is not dead

BE YOURSELF BECAUSE SOME
HAS TO AND YOURE THE CLOSE

"IF WE DO NOT CHANGE OUR COURSE WE WILL END UP WHERE WE ARE GOING."

MASS

Here

Done

back and forth between the north and south stages, so, acting in unison, they carved out trails through the trees and brush. Now people could

NEW YORK

best performance of Woodstock '94. The punk trio was bursting with energy, like preschoolers who had eaten too much Halloween candy

inger/guitarist Billie Joe Armstrong stalked around the stage, bassist Mike Dirnt kept leaping into the air as if he couldn't obey the law of grav-

ity a second longer and drummer Tré Cool kept the beat loud and strong. They blazed through the pissed-off strains of "Chump" and the thro

Green Day (from left): Billie Joe Armstrong, Mike Dirnt, Tré Cool

g bass groove of "Longview," and within minutes they had gotten into a full-scale dirt war with the crowd. Billie Joe taunted members of the

1:45

1:46

@ woodstock·13.64: TJ (WELL3) Sun 14 Aug 94 13:56
As of Sunday afternoon, the clear winner of the Best Band
Show was Green Day. The south stage crowd waited for them
for hours, and when the stage was rotated after W.O.M.A.D
the boys were ready. The crowd went fully berserk. Green
played great music, but soon an incredible mud storm over
whelmed the stage, forcing cameramen to run for cover. As
moshers swept toward the stage, anarchy was near and a ri
seemed imminent. But the security hung tough, the bass pl
er got a cut lip, and the energy typical of a '90s show--r
1969--dominated.

mosh pit ("That guy with the green hair – he thinks he's a punk rocker!"), gave everyone the finger and put the clods of dirt that were thrown

1:58

n into his mouth. At one point he mooned the audience and then turned around and gave them a full-frontal view of Billie Joe, Jr. Soon the

GREE
&
$
#
GRAY
DAY
GREEN

stage was slick with mud, and fans were charging past the security guards to accost the band. The stage divers were playful, but threatenir

MIKE DIRNT'S WOODSTOCK EXPERIENCE

ENTERING WOODSTOCK I HAD A PRECONCEPTION OF HIPPIES EVERYWHERE COMING BACK TO FIND THE ONES THEY HAD LOST IN '69. IT SEEMED A BIT INCONSEQUENTIAL IN THE LONG STREAM OF 1994, AND THE YEAR WAS NOWHERE NEAR OVER (STILL ISN'T). SO WE TOOK IT AS ANOTHER GIG. SO AFTER ALL THE TICKETS WERE SOLD AND PEOPLE DECIDED THEY JUST WEREN'T GOING TO TAKE NO FOR AN ANSWER, WE THOUGHT WHAT KIND OF WAR ZONE WERE THEY TAKING US TO? ATLANTA ONE DAY WITH LOLLAPALOOZA; ONE PLANE, FOUR CARS, ONE BOAT AND TWO HELICOPTERS LATER, THEY DROPPED US SMACK DAB IN THE MIDDLE OF OH...SAY...TWO, MAYBE THREE HUNDRED THOUSAND PEOPLE--AHHHHHH! SEEING THOUSANDS OF PEOPLE LEAVING BY FOOT, WITHOUT A SINGLE SMILE, WAS ONE INDICATION OF WHO WE WERE GOING TO BE PLAY-ING FOR. WE WENT PRETTY MUCH STRAIGHT TO THE SOUTH STAGE. THE CROWD WAS GETTING QUITE ROWDY. RIGHT AS WE TOOK THE STAGE, THE MUD-FILLED GRASS/HAY STARTED FLYING. WITHIN THIRTY MINUTES WE HAD MANAGED TO COME ACROSS AS A FUN-FILLED VENT FOR A LOT OF MUDSTOCK VICTIMS' FRUSTRATIONS, AND IN THE COURSE OF EVENTS BECAME VICTIMS OURSELVES. WE LEFT IN A BIT OF A RUSH DUE TO A SECURITY GUARD PLAYING FOOTBALL WITH ME ONSTAGE (OUCH!), BUT BETTER ME THAN SOME KID OUT THERE. WE MANAGED TO PLAY HALF OF OUR INTENDED SET, AND TO DESTROY THE SOUTH STAGE IN THE PROCESS. ALL IN ALL, IT WAS PROBABLY THE CLOSEST THING TO TOTAL ANARCHY I'LL EVER SEE. I'M GLAD I WAS ABLE TO BE PART OF SUCH CHAOS. WAS IT A GOOD IDEA?

YOU DECIDE.

2:07

ke a guy twirling a toy gun as a presidential motorcade passes by, they had to be dealt with; it was getting too wild to continue. A scuffle broke

2:11

out between the members of Green Day and a security guard and then the show was over. (Later, Green Day's manager would tell me th

peace

ssist Dirnt lost a few teeth – apparently a security guard mistook him for a stage-diving fan). Woodstock '94 had actually managed to have a

W woodstock.4.74: gimme an "F"! (reva) Sun 14 Aug 94 21:49
I'm amazed by the energy and the activity level here!

W woodstock.15.78: Sagerer (WELL3) Sun 14 Aug 94 14:37
Loretta Mower (maiden), take care of the Chameleon's
Heidi--I left her in the pit to deal with Green Day.
Mom, Dad and gang, hope you are groovin' like me!!!

surreal

truly punk show. > > > After Green Day finished, the crowd acted as one again. It wanted to get to the north stage, but the opening in the w

field

Schedule

On the Street

Hot Stories

gate was too small to allow more than a few people at a time to pass through. The cry went up: "Rip down the fence!" In tandem, a hundred peo-

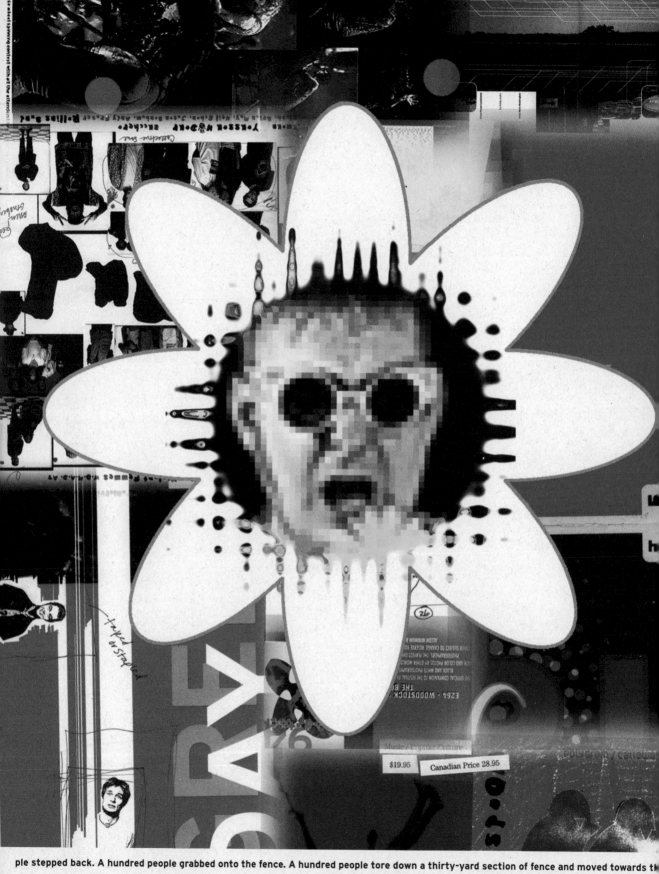

ple stepped back. A hundred people grabbed onto the fence. A hundred people tore down a thirty-yard section of fence and moved towards th

40.87 miles of scaffolding 500 speakers 750,000
00 midnight early brea
200 microphones 15 miles of gui
pe 2,000,000 gallons of
broadcast in over 50 countries 4
4.5 miles of
1.7 acres of stage 550 stage

eco village

over 1,200 medical personnel 2,80
31,250 gallons of coffee
power 250 nine-volt batteries per
fluid ounces of soda 17
miles of scaffolding 500 speakers
helicopters
udio cable 200 microphones 15

acts that day had their moments of brilliance. Arrested Development had the crowd bouncing to Afrocentric hip-hop; Porno for Pyros put on an

of sound 25,000 feet of water
4,960,000 gallons of soda 125,000 pounds of french fries
strings 350 telephones 125,000 pounds of cheese 100,000 woodstock T-shirts
ater 71 miles of hotdogs 3,000 press passes issued
sical acts 29 hours of music
pizzas 100,000 bagels
s 840 acres of land 120 stands

Port-O-Sans over 9 mega-watts
12 tons of ice 67,200,000
200 AA batteries per day 40.87
hospital beds 3 medevac
0,000 watts of sound 12 miles of
ambulances 350 telephones
s of guitar strings

odd circus-rock act that involved lesbian strippers, acrobats and bleeding clowns; and the goof-funk band Red Hot Chili Peppers dressed in

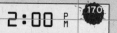

W woodstock.15.61: WATER/alabama (WELLS) Sat 13 Aug 94 07:47 GLASTONBURY?!?!?! Why, the Swedes here said this tops Glastonbury and Pink Pop put together. America's still the world leader in decadent behavior.

traffic

Traffic (from left): Walfredo Reyes, Jim Capaldi, Mike McEvoy, Steve Winwood, Jim Capaldi, Rosko Gee

Devo-like silver uniforms with giant light bulbs on their heads – and during an encore, the entire band came back in fake Afros, in some sort o

Paul Rodgers Rock-Blues Review

Paul Rodgers

Andy Fraser

Slash and Jason Bonham

Neil Schon

Woodstock homage to Hendrix. Despite the Peppers' oddball costume changes, the highlight of their performance was their high-spirited romp

through Stevie Wonder's "Higher Ground," Lead singer Anthony Kiedis asked audience members to remove their shirts and spin them in the ai

It's finally hit me! I've been here about 36 hours and I've got to take my first porta-dump. Lord help me.

...or their heads. The crazy thing was — almost everyone did it! The effect was amazing, a wild Woodstock nation of hundreds of thousands of...

Q: What are you trying to get from and give to Woodstock '94?

Chris Barron: You can't go to the future without embracing the past for what it truly is. I think the '60s did not fail the way some people say it did. I think it put the word peace into people's minds and hearts permanently, hopefully.

Spin Doctors

TCR 21:54:48.02
PLAY   LOCK

at higher ground earlier that afternoon — marijuana use was open and widespread. One guy was going around with a sign that said he was

THE nevi

looking for drugs (between you and me I think he was five-o). > > >   The two performances that seem to sum up the night and Woodst

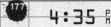

Q: What is this Woodstock about for you?

Aaron Neville: You can't recreate the past. This is a new day. There are new people and a new vision on the world. One thing that is the same is that we still... sang "Amazing Grace" and it just got to everybody out there. It's twenty-five years... and there's... made again, and we're part of it.

lle BROTHERS

porno

FOR

...he sun was beginning to set, the anticipation became almost unbearable. It was then that Dylan, the veteran showman, stepped onto center-

stage – his timing was perfect. He had the same golden light on him that had so effectively enhanced Crosby, Stills and Nash's performance t

day before. Dylan was in fine voice and spirits. He's not always a giving performer, but today he seemed to want to please. He had missed the

original Woodstock, and he was going to make his presence felt at this one. He played a few of his best-known songs, including a rocking "A

Along The Watchtower" and a ravishing, emotional "Just Like A Woman." Dylan even threw in "Everybody Must Get Stoned," a pro-pot anthem

ⓦ woodstock.15.76: no
There's nutti
drugged-out f
to the stage.

that the Cypress Hill set could identify with.　>>>　English rocker Peter Gabriel closed the concert. He kept saying, "This is you

(WELL3) Sun, 14 Aug 94 08:19
but a bunch of
aks when you get up

Woodstock," to the crowd. He played a range of old and new material – the American Indian-themed song "San Jacinto," the cathartic rocker

Q: Is this just about nostalgia? Shouldn't these people be looking ahead for new music and culture like the first Woodstock audience?

Carlos Santana: Peace and love is fine but without the music you and I would not be here. People come here because the music is a sound that goes inside their hearts and makes their hair stand up and is more than they're getting outside.

"Red Rain," the chart-topping "Sledgehammer" and "In Your Eyes," a song inflected with African rhythms. He added a few interesting mod-

It's kind of like **HARMO-NIOUS CONVER-GENCE PART 2...** it because it's worth it to be exalted by a something that might change your life.

carlos Santana

Q: What do you think Hendrix would say if he were back here today looking at all these people?

Jimmy Cliff: He'd say, "Man, here we are again, man. I hope we are growing. I hope we are getting along."

JIMMY CLIFF'S
Reggae Jam
featuring Diana King, Worl-A-Girl, Toots, Eek-A-Mouse

with song titles like "Moribund The Burgermeister" and album covers that showed his face melting. He was alternative before there was an

alternative. Now he's a Grammy winner, an eld   sman of rock and mainstream.   > > >   And so is Woodstock. And that's why Gabri

If you look
up into the sky,
you'll find
yourself standing
in eternity."

Allen Ginsberg

W

woodstock.3b.8:cerise(WELL) Sun 14 Aug 94 17:51

Amazing sunset! A fitting atmospheric lead-in for Bob Dylan going on the
north stage. Really cooling off now; smell of campfires in the air....

"a" word again — alternative. "This is your Woodstock," he kept saying. At the end of his set, he had the crowd light candles and sing alon

"Biko," his tribute song to Stephen Biko, the slain black South African activist. >>> Woodstock was over. It was dark and cold, and the

Bob

mud was getting hard. The rave was still going on, and it would go on until very, very late that night, but Woodstock was over. There were

8:00 P M

woodstock.15.19: woodman (WELLS) Thu 11 Aug 94 17:03
I have been experiencing flashbacks from the original experience
(I was 16 in 1969) and am struck by how similar this Woodstock feels to the
original. The field, the grass, the stage, the weather. It's curious and
exciting. The similarities and differences in the times and generations. . .

Dylan

closed my eyes, and I could still see a landscape of candles.   > > >   After Gabriel finished, many people seemed almost lost. Some were I

ally lost, wandering the wrong way down the road in the dark as they trekked back to their cars or hotels. Others held up signs looking to

hitch rides to places like Ohio, Georgia and Vermont. Post-Woodstock, in the glare of the morning, some of the Mud People looked a littl

mbarrassed to be so dirty – yesterday they were a nation; today, they were back to being individual states of confusion. The Trailways bus station offered a free hose-down. Other Woodstock attendees simply refused to leave, lurking around the debris of the concert, whic

9:15 P M

included a surfboard and, reportedly, the box for a kit to make a two-person boat (where the boat ended up is anyone's guess). Woodstock

woodstock.30.17:Fumihiko "Miko" Matsumura (miko) Sun 14 Aug 94 23:38
I was in the mosh pit front and center during Red Hot Chili Peppers.
Flea told everyone to take off their shirts and twirl them,
and practically everyone did.

was over, finished, done. Stick a fork in it. > > > But Woodstock wasn't over. Not really. There's this Woody Allen movie that you probably

Red Hot Chili Pepper Anthony Kiedis

ver saw where a character asks, rhetorically, "Is a memory something you have or something you've lost?" The music world is split into a

million different factions. Punk, funk, folk, metal, techno, rap, gangsta rap, bebop, hip-hop, and those genres split fans apart, too. They go to

separate shows, have separate experiences, go their separate ways. Woodstock cut through all that. You may not have liked all of it, you peter

may not have liked any of it, but everyone was having a common experience; together, everyone was muddy, miserable, happy or hung-ov

or three days. And now we all have the same memories of Woodstock. They may differ on the specifics, but they're essentially the same.

woodstock.23.15: edmon (WELL) Fri 12 Aug 94 19:07
As I was leaving Peter Gabriel's, candles were being lit crowd-wide for Rwanda. It was the best birthday cake ever (I turned 26 today, Aug 14, the last day of Woodstock!)

>>> Is a memory something you have or something you've lost?

Whichever it is, I don't think anyone who was there will ever forget.

We'll always have Saugerties. > > > Christopher John Farley

sleep

w woodstock.29.21: Nick Ripple Cichanowski (WELL3) Fri
Born free, live free, peace to all, and good luck to all
still outside the wall to freedom.

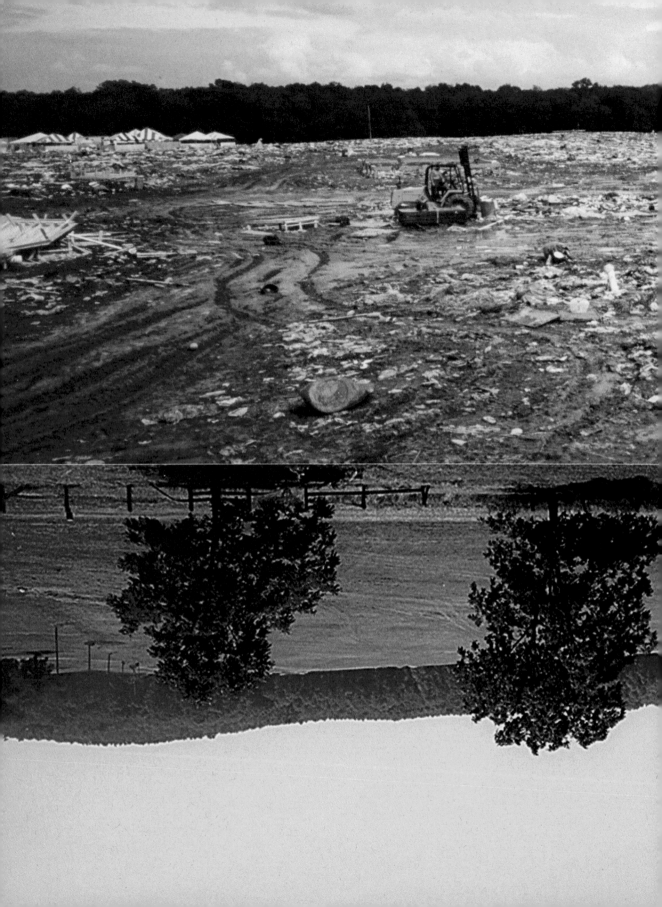

From the Producers

We have always believed that Woodstock means more than a rock n' roll concert. Woodstock is a state of mind that is not confined by the boundaries of a field, or typified by a musical genre or locked into any particular period of time. While Woodstock '69 may have come to define a generation in the minds of some, in our view Woodstock represents a longing in the hearts of people to connect with one another by sharing an experience where anything is possible.

What was created in 1969 has been recreated, in essence and in spirit, twenty-five years later in 1994. As festivals, Woodstock '69 and Woodstock '94 each gave voice to the distinct historical frameworks in which they were set. Drawn together by the music, moved by the faces of so many assembled and exhilarated by the temporary discomforts of rain and mud, the vast crowd celebrated and then left with a sense of wholeness and unity that is inherent in the legend which has come to be known as "Woodstock."

As the producers of Woodstock, we were called upon to assemble a production team, battle the politics, find the money, figure the logistics and calculate the risks while protecting the spirit. But, after all is said and done, it is the audience who are the real creators of and spokespersons for these monumental events. What we have been fortunate enough to contribute is a place, a time and a means for those who are drawn away from their daily lives by the mystique of "Woodstock" — to a farm in Saugerties — to create a legacy of peace and music again...and again.

Michael Lang

John Roberts

Joel Rosenman

John Scher

Producer	**Ivan Wong, Jr.**
Editor	**Andrea Danese**
Creative Directors	**Michael Rock and Susan Sellers**
Designers	**Hsein-Yin Chou, Ebon Heath, Michael Rock**
	Susan Sellers, Georgianna Stout
Assistant Designers	**Toshiya Masuda, Christian Küsters**
Director of Photography	**Karen Mullarkey**
Director of Production	**True Sims**
Director of Digital Production	**Jeremy M. Sherber**
Technical Consultant	**Richard Benson**
Digital Pre-Press Advisor	**Mark Boyer**
Assistant to the Producer	**John McCormick**
Editorial Director	**Nicholas Callaway**
Director of Sales and Marketing	**Paula Litzky**
Legal Counsel to Callaway	**Paul Schindler**
PolyGram Book Coordinator	**Tom Bennett**
Assistant PolyGram Book Coordinator	**Karen Barwick**

Albert Watson served as the official portrait photographer Woodstock '94. All black-and-white portraits of the performers, as well as members of the audienc were photographed by Albert Watson. A backstage tent functioned as Watson's studio at the festiva The images that appear in the Woodstock Mud Person Flip-Book (pages 87-123) are courtesy Woodstock '94: The Film, **produced and directed by Barbara Kopple. Amy Wu, 19, is a student and a free** lance writer who covered Woodstock '94 for People. The text by Amy Wu that appears in this book wa reprinted with the permission of Gannett Suburban Newspapers. **John Milward, a freelance writer an** critic, wrote about Woodstock '94 for The Los Angeles Times and Rolling Stone. **Christopher John Farle** is a staff writer for Time **magazine. His article about Woodstock '94 appeared in** Time **magazine tw** weeks after the event. Interviews with the performers were conducted backstage at Woodstock '94 b Aaron Watson. Excerpts from these interviews appear either as quotes or in a question-and-answe format. Scott Osman (aka Scotto) was one of the coordinators of Ravestock. Excerpts from the confe ences and digital postings that were entered onto the WELL on-site at Woodstock '94 are feature throughout this book. All excerpts from the WELL are introduced by the WELL symbol along with th digital posting of each entry. 35mm color transparency scans, color-correction and cropping wer completed via the Digital Link Gateway System by Applied Graphics Technologies, Digital Imagin Systems Division.

colophon

Woodstock '94 was published by Polygram Diversified Entertainment and Callaway Editions. The book was designed and produced by Michael Rock.Susan Sellers Partners in New York City. The entire book - from initial creative meetings to press - was accomplished during the eight weeks immediately following the festival. The book is the result of a close collaboration between PolyGram, Callaway, designers, writers, photographers, technicians and the Woodstock '94 producers. Photo editor Karen Mullarkey sifted through over 2,000 rolls of film (72,000 35mm slides) in four days. With only 48 hours turnaround allotted, AGT's Digital Imaging System Division was responsible for digitizing, annotating and color-correcting nearly 400 35mm color transparencies. Using DISD's digital Link Gateway System, the images were digitized at very high resolutions, color-corrected, cropped, and then exported as TIFF images for final conversions to CMYK. Albert Watson's black-and-white portraits were separated for process color by Richard Benson and Daniel Benson at Benson's studio in Newport, Rhode Island. Design and layout was performed by a team of five designers working simultaneously on Apple Macintosh Power PCs using QuarkXpress™ 3.3 and Adobe Photoshop™ 3.0 on seven workstations linked with EtherWave™ networking system provided by Farallon Computing, Inc. Tom Reilly of Radius Inc. was the generous providor of SuperMac™ SuperMatch™ 21 T XL Super-Res Color Display Monitors, SuperMatch™ Display Calibrator Pros, Thunder II™ GX 1360 color graphic accelerator cards, VideoVision Studio and SuperMatch™ Proof-Positive Two-Page Printers to the project. Without this vital technical support, the book would never have been completed in record time. Jeremy M. Sherber presided over all digital pre-press and production. The files containing the book layouts and images were stored and transported on SledgeHammer™ and JackHammer™ disk arrays, which were loaned by Tom Fristo at FWB®, Inc. Jonathan Caponi of Adobe Systems Incorporated assisted in the digital production, video capturing and editing of video footage that was provided by the Woodstock '94 news team and Barbara Kopple, the producer and director of Woodstock '94: The Film. Two original typefaces were designed for Woodstock '94: the sans serif Saugerties by Tobias Frere-Jones and the serif Courtjester by Christian Küsters. Other fonts include Frere-Jones' REACTOR and Interstate, and Cornel Windlin's Moserdischk. Woodstock '94 is printed on recycled paper in process color by RR Donnelley & Sons Company in Willard, Ohio, under the supervision of Richard Benson and Toshiya Masuda. Special thanks to Jackie Barndollar and Jay Shutts of RR Donnelley & Sons Company. Thanks also to Irma Boom.

Ph⚬t⚬ cṛedits

Acknowledgments

THE PRODUCERS Michael Lang John Roberts Joel Rosenman John ...er THE EVENT BOARD Ossie Kilkenny Eric Kronfeld Michael Lang John Scher THE OPERATIONS GROUP Tom ...rana/Associate Producer Ken Graham/Site Manager Hector Lizzardi/Site Coordinator Jake Kennedy Bob Koch THE STAFF ...Ferdinand Anderson/Medical Director Ana Luisa Anjosi/Director of Performance Artists Tess Arevalo/PolyGram Public Relations Vrej ...ghoomian/Associate Director of Murals Terresa Bakner/Legal Counsel Karen Barwick/Assistant to Tom Bennett Keith Beccia/Construc- ...n & Concession Consultant Tom Bennett/Project Merchandiser Michael Berg/Family of Woodstock Lee Blumer/Executive Assistant to ...chael Lang Brenda Brady/Executive Assistant to Jeff Rowland Allen Branton/Lighting Designer Dawn Bridges/PolyGram Public Rela- ...ns Jennifer Brody/Public Relations Assistant Aileen Budow/Publicity Matthew Burgher/Surveyor Robert Burgher/Engineer Pamela ...rton/Credentials John Campion/Show Power Chris Cooke/Security John Conmy/Scrip Joe Costa/Concessions General Manager Bill ...wen/Assistant to John Roberts Pete D'Auria/Finance Anthony Davis/Security Herb Decordova/Licensing David DeForrest/Lead Hospi- ...Coordinator Danny DeSilverstro/Security Ken Deranleau/Stage Manager Duke Devlin/Media Site Tour Director, Official Archivist Robert ...G. Disney/Director of Security, Safety and Flight Operations Renee Dossick/Legal Affairs Kevin Drescher/Project Planner for Saugerties ...lice Force Robin Ellis/Production Assistant Sharon Ericksen/Executive Assistant to Tom Cyrana Mike Esmonde/Lead Stage Manager, ...rth Stage Maria Fabiano/Hospital Coordinator Mike Fallon/Site Coordinator Jim Featherstonhaugh/Special Consultant Mitch Fen- ...l/Surreal Field Site Coordinator Dennis Frank/Concessions Manager Carl Freed/Hotel Coordinator Paulette Garneau/Project Accoun- ...t Bill Georges/Security Consultant Phil Gitlen/Lead Outside Legal Counsel Allan Glickman/Hospital Coordinator Steve Gold/Communi- ...Relations Wayne Goldberg/Talent Coordinator James Golden/Security Richard J. Goldman/Legal Counsel, Medical Susan ...ldman/Family of Woodstock Adam Gottlieb/EMS Coordinator Tammy Grande/Office Manager, Manhattan Office (South) Matthew Gross- ...n/Managing Director Manhattan Office Wendy Harris/Assistant Production Coordinator Harry Herman/Security Rand Hoffman/Poly- ...am Business Affairs Bugsy Houghdahl/Stage Manager (South) Tom Hudak/Press, VIP Site Coordinator Steve Iredale/Production Man- ...er (North) Paul Kallush/Merchandising Sales Director Firat Kasapoglu/Assistant Site Manager Patricia Kiel/PolyGram Public Rela- ...ns Corliss Kitchens/Executive Assistant to John Scher Michael Klenfner/Stage Security Spiritual Advisor Dan Klores/Publicity Lee ...ife/Legal Affairs Jim Koplik/Associate Producer Artie Kornfeld/Founding Father Michael Kushner/Woodstock Project Business Affairs ...riann Lang/Local Talent Coordinator Shala Lang/Local Talent Coordinator Martin Leffer/Craft Village Coordinator Steve Lemon/Project ...nager, Production Coordinator Ron Leonard/Co-Coordinator EcoVillage Jane Lipsitz/Co-Associate Producer, Marketing Dean Long/LA ...oup Chuck Manning/Transportation Ilene Marder/Public Relations Ron Martinelli/Manager, Telecommunications Jim McCafferty/Scrip ...gene MacDonald/Security Jim McDonald/Talent Coordinator Joe McFadden/Site Finance Tom McPhillips/Scenic Designer Greg Mor- ...n/Merchandising Production Director Lloyd Morrison/Controller John Morrison/Production Manager (South) Mo Morrison/Executive in ...arge of Production Helen Murphy/Treasurer Barbara Naccarato/Hospital Coordinator Frances Nestler/Office Manager Allen ...wman/Producer, Television Debbie Newman/Talent Coordinator Larry Offsey/Finance Paul O'Connell/Deputy Director of Security Opera- ...ns Joe O'Herlihy/Audio Designer John O'Rourke/Director of Fire Safety Adam Palter/Merchandising Artwork Coordinator Susan ...papaschalis/Site Receptionist Donna Parise/Assistant to Paulette Garneau Dan Parise/Production John Pelosi/Legal Affairs Barbara ...nsoy/Director, Mural Project Mike Peragine/Executive Helicopter Russ Pittenger/LA Group David Polk/Security Jonathan Quitt/Sur- ...al Field Tim Rabbett/Manager, Off Site Security The Rainbow Family/Campgrounds Deborah Rathwell/Talent Coordinator Al ...bhun/Merchandising, Production Coordinator Rick Rentz/Security David Reuss/Artist Transportation Martin Ricciardi/Legal Counsel ...ug Roberts/Assistant to Hector Lizzardi Rona Roberts/Crisis Intervention Al Rosenthal/Risk Management Lisa Rothblum/Legal Affairs ...ff Rowland/Associate Producer Emily Rubin/Public Relations Greta Rucker/Merchandising Promotional Coordinator Paul ...hindler/Legal Counsel Robin Schmalback/Scrip, Finance Nancy Schmidt/Transportation James Schmidt/Transportation Michael ...ltzer/Legal Affairs Philip Shienbein/Transportation Danny Socolof/Surreal Field Producer Cap Spence/Director, Artist Transportation ...l Spielman/Financial Advisor Mike Stock/Construction Manager Hayley Sumner/Publicity Julie Swidler/Legal Affairs George Terpen- ...g/Community Affairs Bill Thiel/Deputy Director of Security, Logistics Jeremy Thom/Stage Manager (North) Torben Torp-Smith/Con- ...ruction Supervisor Frank Turk/Construction Supervisor Ken Viola/Manager, Stage Security George Walden/Insurance Mark ...alker/Legal Affairs David Weiss/EcoVillage Coordinator Joe Wirsing/Stage Manager (North) Lenny Wohl/Legal Affairs Steve Yeager/Car- ...ntry Coordinator Jim Young/Land Acquisition Danny Zausner/Ticketing Ariel Zevon/Generation Xposition, Youth Movement Crystal ...von/Executive Assistant to Michael Lang

THANKS to the following individuals: Daniel Alfonso/Chairman, Ulster County Legislature Kevin Cahill/Assemblyman John ...rashko/Special Laison, Governor Cuomo's Office Dan Flynn/Consultant Jim Griffis/Saugerties Town Supervisor Maurice Hinchey/N.Y. ...ate Congressman Jack Ingersoll/Consultant Lt. Col. James D. O'Donnell/Liaison with N.Y. State Police Dean Palen/Ulster County ...alth Commissioner Wes Pomeroy/Consultant

SPECIAL THANKS to the residents of Saugerties, the Schaller Family and Dr. Masood Ansari

(W) The WELL (Whole Earth 'Lectronic Link) is on
of the most established and eclectic on-line conferencing communities in the world. The WEL
offers hundreds of conferences on topics ranging from virtual reality and gardening to jazz
and Generation X. The WELL is also a full-service Internet access provider. At Woodstock
'94, the WELL gave concertgoers a historic presence on the Internet and made it possible fo
people off-site to participate in the event electronically. Using the latest Internet technologies, people at Woodstock '94 were able to sign into a Digital Scrapbook to post their
thoughts, pictures and even audio clips live from the event. This conference was open to the
entire Internet community, in real time, and provided a forum for lively, untethered discus-
sion. To become a member of the WELL, or for more information, send email to: info@well.com
or call 1.415.332.4335 for a special Woodstock offer. Woodstock '94's digital history
remains archived and can be accessed by those on the World Wide Web at the following URL
address: http:/ /www.well.com/woodstock/